THE
WORKING RAILWAY

a railwayman's photographs 1960·67

volume 1

RON HERBERT

Silver Link Publishing

5 HAWK STREET, CARNFORTH, LANCASHIRE, LA5 9LA.

ACKNOWLEDGEMENTS

PUTTING this book together has been a thoroughly enjoyable task, and selecting the 168 photographs for inclusion in the following pages prompted many happy memories both of my work and my railway photography. Although my name appears on this book, it would never have appeared without the help and support of many people and I would like to acknowledge their assistance here. First of all I would like to thank my colleagues on the railway past and present – especially those in Control – for their professional expertise and help. Without the invaluable aid of my friends in Traffic Control in particular some of the pictures which follow simply would not have been possible. I would also like to say a hearty word of thanks to Derek Mercer, of Morden, Surrey, for producing such outstanding prints from my negatives, many of which are now 20 years old.

Finally, my sincere thanks to Silver Link Publishing for all the help and encouragement in guiding me through the business of compiling a book – a new experience for me – and for aiming for the highest quality at every stage. It was a great team effort and I hope that SLP is as pleased with the finished product as I am!

CONTENTS

4 .... Introduction
8 .... Lancaster
24 .... The Glasson Dock Branch
27 .... North of Lancaster
30 .... Hest Bank
36 .... Bare Lane, Morecambe
40 .... Morecambe Euston Road
42 .... Carnforth
48 .... East to Hellifield
50 . Carnforth-Carlisle: Main Line and branches
58 .... Mixed Traffic
60 .... York
64 .... On Shed
66 .... Scotland
68 .... Wales
72 .... Southern Steam
76 .... The Isle of Wight
78 .... Evercreech Junction
80 .... The Isle of Man
83 .... Bromsgrove
84 .... Ireland
90 .... Spain & Italy
92 .... France & Germany
94 .. The Romney, Hythe & Dymchurch Railway

OPPOSITE PAGE: Riddles 'Britannia' Pacific No. 70052 *Firth of Tay* forges up the bank south of Lancaster with a Glasgow Central-Euston relief (1X77), July 6 1963.

PREVIOUS PAGE: Ivatt 2MT 2-6-0 No. 46441 approaches Bare Lane, Morecambe with the 4.55pm Lakeside-Morecambe Promenade of July 2 1965.

FRONT COVER: Stanier 8F 2-8-0 No. 48319 hauls an engineers special from Heysham tip to Northampton across the level crossing at Bare Lane, Morecambe, at 11am on January 24 1964. I didn't have to go far to take pictures like this, as my father was Station Master at Bare Lane and I lived there from 1956 until 1971. My interest in railways must have sprung from my father's dedication and enthusiasm for his job.

BACK COVER: A crew change at Stirling on May 10 1965, as Stanier 5MT 4-6-0 No. 45168 waits to leave with the 6.15am Oban-Edinburgh Waverley service.

INTRODUCTION

IT'S a common enough saying that railways are 'in the blood' but it was certainly true in my case, for my father was not only a professional railwayman, but also a knowledgeable railway enthusiast. His interest in railways was very deep indeed and he never went anywhere without his much-thumbed copy of the 'Bradshaw' timetable.

I suppose it was therefore inevitable that this interest would rub off, and sure enough, it did. I can well recall childhood holidays which were always taken at a location which could be classed as a holiday centre — but which, more importantly, were railway centres of great interest. From my father's base, then at Chester, we travelled in the 1950s to Scarborough, Gourock, Bournemouth and Bangor (County Down), all of which seemed to me at the time to be far away places!

One of my first memories of such a holiday was travelling from Prestatyn, our home, to Heysham Harbour in the summer of 1950 to join the SS Duke of Lancaster for the night sailing to Belfast, en route to Bangor. We left Belfast Queens Quay the following morning behind a B&CW R 4-4-2T, the first of many steam-hauled runs in Northern Ireland which were to extend through to the late 1960s. These were some of my happiest days in pursuit of steam traction with my companions and camera. There is no doubt that this early introduction to Irish railways prompted me to make the crossing of the Irish Sea on numerous occasions for the next 17 years. It was a marvellous system — a superb example of the working railway of the steam era.

In 1953 my father was transferred from Chester to Carnforth as a Relief Station Master, covering the area from Leyland to Penrith, and including the Windermere and Keswick branches. This was the turning point in my growing interest in railways, for having been used to the smooth running of steam on the North Wales Coast, or the sight of trains ambling down the many branches in the area, I was suddenly plunged into a railway full of Anglo Scottish expresses hauled by majestic Stanier Class 8P 'Pacifics', 'Britannia' Pacifics, 'Royal Scot' and 'Patriot' 4-6-0s, unlimited numbers (it seemed!) of Stanier 'Black 5s' — also Riddles 'Clan' Pacifics which always appeared to have a Fowler Class 2 4-4-0 attached in front as a pilot engine!

Every time you approached Carnforth station the up and down loops would be full of freight trains awaiting train crew relief or a path onto the main line behind one of the many passenger trains. It was a busy, bustling scene which drew me like a magnet and it was then that I realised that I wanted to be a part of this working railway when I left school.

At last, on April 21 1958 I began my railway career on British Railways at Lancaster Castle station, training as a telegraph clerk. It is hard to believe as I look back to those days that all telegrams and train reporting was conducted in morse code, devices such as tele-printers being unheard of at Lancaster! Part of the duties of the Telegraph section was to report to the Control at Preston, who would be informed of the passing times of trains at selected locations. This was my first contact with Control and like my colleagues, I treated them with the greatest respect. I was at last part of the working railway and I was enjoying every minute of it. I also became much more aware of the details of train working and in February 1960 I bought a Zeiss Werra 35mm camera so I could begin to record the everyday scene as I saw it operate. Thus began my serious railway photography, which was to continue for the next seven years.

In April of that year I travelled on a Manchester Locomotive Society/Stephenson Locomotive Society railtour from Lancaster Castle to Glasson Dock and then on to Penrith via Lancaster Castle, Green Ayre, Clapham, Ingleton and Shap. We then continued to Kirkby Stephen East, via Appleby East and returned to Lancaster Castle via Ravenstonedale, Tebay, Arnside, Ulverston and the Lakeside branch. Looking at the railway map of today, bearing this route in mind, is a revealing exercise.

In June I made my first of many visits to the Isle of Man with my father, and fellow enthusiasts Noel Machell and Eddie Crawshaw. Runs over the complete network to Peel, Port Erin and Ramsay were all achieved, including a visit to Douglas shed and works, where enthusiasts were not normally welcome. The IOMR was an idyllic scene, especially for the railway photographer, and I went back many times.

During 1961 many trips were arranged on lines long since closed, such as the Peterhead and Fraserborough branches and the St. Combs Light Railway, steam to Ballachulish, Brecon to Neath, Bath Green Park to Templecombe, the Fowey and Helston branches, Bodmin Road to Wadebridge, Bude, Halwill Junction to Barnstaple via the Torrington Light Railway. I also made my first of many visits to the Isle of Wight, which featured a superb, largely Victorian steam worked railway. The latter part of the summer saw my two friends and I in north and central Wales, photographing the narrow gauge lines, and more importantly, steam on the Cambrian. August brought a further highlight with the MLS/SLS 'Furness Railtour' which ran over many lines, long since closed to passengers at the time: the North Lonsdale branch, Dalton to Stainton Quarry, Ormsgill Junction, to Buccleuch Dock, the Peel branch, Barrow shipyard station, the Hodbarrow branch from Millom and the beautiful Coniston branch from Foxfield.

The year 1962 dawned with a sad run aboard the 10.52am DMU from Penrith to Workington, on the last day of through passenger services on the 'Cockermouth, Keswick & Penrith' line. This trip was made with my father and Derrick Codling, a colleague and another keen railway photographer.

The Divisional Operating Superintendent's Control Office, Preston, at 3.30am on August 5 1962. The Controllers in this room supervised the West Coast Main Line from Euxton to Carnforth, and its branches to Blackpool Central, Blackpool North, Fleetwood, Pilling, Longridge, Morecambe and Heysham. It also controlled the Midland line from Snaygill (near Skipton) to Settle Junction and its branches to Carnforth and Lancaster Green Ayre, and from Clapham Junction to Ingleton. The ex-Lancashire & Yorkshire Railway section from Preston to Copy Pit summit was also controlled from here. These Controllers were responsible for the smooth operation of all passenger and freight workings and the allocation of locomotives and train crews — in addition to the endless stream of unexpected crises and emergencies that each shift invariably brought.

In March of that year a most important change took place in my railway career. I was summoned to Preston to be interviewed by the District Operating Superintendent and some days later I was advised that I would shortly be transferred to Traffic Control and start training as an Assistant Controller. So began my Control career, which was to continue for many years. I soon became aware that 'the Control' was the focal point of all train operation in the area and with the aid of my new colleagues I was soon being advised which locomotives were working specific trains, and of any unusual movements that were being arranged — official or otherwise! Consequently, my Zeiss Werra became standard equipment to take to work, as the opportunities were endless and extremely varied. Control was an exacting, but incredibly satisfying job and I look back very happily on this period. Each shift brought its share of crises and emergencies, but this ensured lots of interest, and gave the individual the chance to prove his ability. It was a job of great professionalism and friendly comradeship with your colleagues. Control was the hub of railway operation and required maximum concentration and commitment, but it was not without its lighter moments, as one of the accompanying pictures shows!

At this time, Beeching's cuts were fast approaching and the main holiday that summer was spent photographing the remaining 'King' 4-6-0s on Hatton bank, in addition to the Bulleid 'Pacifics' on the Waterloo-Salisbury-Bournemouth lines. Some time was spent on the S&DJR line and on the last day of our tour we visited Bromsgrove, at the foot of the Lickey Incline. Happy days. Once again, a railtour completed a most successful year. It was organised by the Railway Correspondence & Travel Society and began at the Fishergate Hill station, in Preston, and ran to Grassington via Longridge, Padiham and Colne, and returning via Blackburn, Cherry Tree and Chorley.

1963 began with interesting train movements in the Lancaster & Morecambe area caused by the reconstruction of Lune Bridge ('Carlisle Bridge') at Lancaster, and for two weekends the main line services were diverted via Bare Lane, Morecambe, Lancaster Green Ayre and via the steep single line to Lancaster Castle. It was a photographer's dream come true. In July I changed my long serving Werra for a Rolleicord, armed with which I made further visits to Northern Ireland, the Isle of Wight and the Isle of Man to complete another successful year in search of steam.

At the beginning of 1964 I changed my camera again, this time buying a Rolleiflex, and in March I photographed Fowler 2-6-4T No. 42301 at Glasson Dock, en route to the local shipbreakers yard, for cutting up. This was the only occasion a locomotive was cut up at Glasson Dock. A visit to Northern Ireland followed which included a footplate trip over the border to Dundalk on a Class 'WT' 2-6-4T. In May I returned home and spent as much time as I could at the trackside on the branch lines, which Beeching was now closing so quickly that it was impossible to get to many of them in time.

May also brought Riddles 'Clan' Pacific No. 72007 *Clan Mackintosh* to Lancaster Penny Street station on the RCTS Ribble Lune Railtour — a sight never to be forgotten. Another RCTS railtour took place on the Glasson Dock branch during June, when an Ivatt 2MT 2-6-0 hauled a train of brake vans over its five-mile length.

September 1964 brought the fateful day when No. 46256 *Sir William A Stanier FRS* worked its last day in service on the RCTS 'Scottish Lowlander' railtour and thus brought the era of the Stanier Pacifics on the WCML to an end. It was a sad day and I realised the end was near. In 1965, I thus travelled north to see the Gresley A4 Pacifics on the Aberdeen-Glasgow services — another never to be forgotten sight.

In May of 1965 I went to France to see SNCF steam in action between Calais and Amiens, followed by a trip to another old favourite, the Romney Hythe and Dymchurch Railway. Before the end of the year I managed to fit in a trip to Germany to see DB steam at work, and squeezed in shed visits to Munich, Mannheim, Stuttgart and Koblenz.

Time was running out fast in 1966 and it was a case of trying to fit in as much as possible before the end came. It was a time of 'last days' and 'last trains' as lines, stations and sheds closed and steam steadily faded away in grime and neglect. The year's highlights included visits to the Isle of Wight, a high-speed run behind an A4 between Glasgow and Aberdeen, and a trip to Bournemouth and Weymouth to pay homage to the Bulleid 'Pacifics', while Autumn brought a holiday in Eire, returning home via Belfast and Larne in order to photograph the remaining Class WT 2-6-4Ts.

1967 was the end, and with my Rollei I began my last year of railway photography. January took me to Sicily to see the remaining FS steam locomotives, while in May I was back to Northern Ireland to photograph the WT 2-6-4T No. 10 and GSR 0-6-0 No. 186 on a Railway Preservation Society of

Train Control was definitely a serious and professional business — but it was not without its lighter moments! Here we see the scene at Preston Control at 9am on Sunday July 14 1963. For the sake of the camera and posterity the Controllers that day were (left to right): Harry Miller, Tommy Fletcher, Ian Hall, George Whyatt, Albert Barnes and Gerry Maher. The placards are a mixture of official terminology and control room good humour; WRD (work rest day); SuO (operates Sundays only); and NABF (Never a bare fortnight). This was an oblique reference to the hectic control room roster and the supposed contents of your wage packet!

This was one of my favourite locations for photographing steam — the 1 in 98 southbound climb from Lancaster, on the West Coast Main Line. Stanier 'Black 5' 4-6-0 No. 44883 tackles the grade with the 10.25am Glasgow-Blackpool Central (1M21) of November 2 1964. The leading vehicle is a Gresley BG — at this time pre-nationalisation rolling stock was a regular sight on the WCML on summer Saturdays.

Ireland special on the Portrush branch. Numerous trips to Bournemouth and Weymouth continued until the fateful day of July 8, when Southern steam breathed its last on BR metals. September witnessed a visit to Spain and Portugal to see what was left of RENFE and CP's once large fleet of steam locomotives, by then much depleted.

As I say at the end of this book, operationally in Britain steam had become a real liability and for Traffic Control, August 1968 saw an end to the endless stream of failures, late running and other operating disasters which had been caused by the neglected and run-down engines. The end of steam was a release from a good deal of difficulty in this respect, but it also drew the fires on a period which for me had been a very interesting and photographically rewarding era of the working railway. It was an experience I shall never forget, and I hope the following pictures will convey some of the unique appeal of the working railway. They have certainly rekindled many happy memories for me!

Ron Herbert
Preston
October 1984

LANCASTER

Above: A railway location which no longer exists — Lancaster Penny Street station. This was the original Lancaster & Preston Railway station, which closed to passengers in 1849, but which remained open for freight until the mid-1960s. This train was the RCTS Ribble-Lune railtour, hauled by Riddles 'Clan' Pacific No. 72007 Clan Mackintosh, **on May 23 1964**

Right: Looking south from Lancaster No. 2 signalbox on April 23 1965. Riddles Class 7P6F No. 70034 Thomas Hardy **coasts down the bank towards Lancaster Castle station with IL25 — the 10.10am Euston-Carlisle, composed entirely of Mk. 1 stock. This section today comprises a double-track section with an up goods loop.**

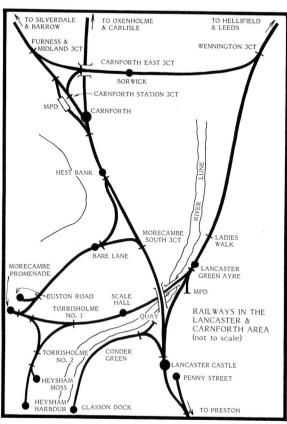

TO SILVERDALE & BARROW
TO OXENHOLME & CARLISLE
TO HELLIFIELD & LEEDS
FURNESS & MIDLAND JCT
WENNINGTON JCT
CARNFORTH EAST JCT
BORWICK
CARNFORTH STATION JCT
MPD
CARNFORTH
HEST BANK
RIVER LUNE
MORECAMBE SOUTH JCT
LADIES WALK
BARE LANE
LANCASTER GREEN AYRE
MORECAMBE PROMENADE
MPD
EUSTON ROAD
SCALE HALL
TORRISHOLME NO. 1
QUAY
RAILWAYS IN THE LANCASTER & CARNFORTH AREA (not to scale)
TORRISHOLME NO. 2
CONDER GREEN
LANCASTER CASTLE
PENNY STREET
HEYSHAM MOSS
HEYSHAM HARBOUR
GLASSON DOCK
TO PRESTON

Left: A southbound Lancaster departure, viewed from the up side of the WCML. Stanier 'Jubilee' 4-6-0 No. 45582 *Central Provinces* heads the 10.35am Carnforth-Warrington freight of June 8 1962. This turn could provide almost anything in the way of motive power.

Above: 'The Duke' at Lancaster. Sole Riddles 8P Pacific No. 71000 *Duke of Gloucester* gets to grips with the southbound climb from Lancaster Castle on February 17 1962 with 3K16, the 8.15am Carlisle-Crewe, known locally as 'The Horse & Carriage.' A sighting of No. 71000 on this section at this time was very rare. The vehicle immediately behind the tender is a Gresley BG.

Riddles Caprotti Class 5 4-6-0 No. 73129, of Patricroft shed, shunts at Lancaster with the 11.42am Milnthorpe-Bay Horse freight of February 7 1962. This locomotive, built in 1956, is now being restored at the Midland Railway Centre, Butterley.

Top: Waiting for the rightaway at Lancaster Castle on March 13 1962 are light-engines (left) Ivatt 4MT 2-6-0 No. 43124 and Ivatt 2MT 2-6-0 No. 46422. The Class 4MT had arrived with the 8.15am parcels from Heysham. The 'live wires' sign to the right refers to the catenary of the Lancaster-Morecambe-Heysham electrified section, which started under the bridge.

Above: Stanier Class 8P Pacific No. 46222 *Queen Mary* comes off the fast line at Lancaster No. 2 signalbox with the 10.5am Glasgow-Birmingham (1M24) of February 7 1962. The up yard behind the 'Pacific' survived in considerably truncated form until summer 1984.

Left: No. 46229 *Duchess of Hamilton,* **now preserved in working order at the National Railway Museum, York, stands at Lancaster Castle on March 16 1962 at the head of the 12.20pm Perth-Euston (1M37).**

Below: A pre-grouping image at Lancaster Castle, as LNWR 'Super D' 0-8-0 No. 49428 ambles north on the down fast line with the 6.25am Ribble Sidings-Heysham Harbour freight, March 19 1961. The building behind the engine is the original Lancaster & Carlisle Railway station of 1849.

This is one of my favourite Stanier Class 8P photographs. No. 46234 *Duchess of Abercorn* passes Lancaster No. 3 signalbox with 2K82 — the 6.20am Carlisle-Crewe — of August 1 1961.

The 3.15pm Windermere-Liverpool Exchange (1K47) of August 5 1961 rolls into Lancaster Castle behind Caprotti 'Black 5' No. 44745. Note the three non-corridor coaches marshalled behind the engine and the marvellous gas lamp on the bridge, above the locomotive.

The northward view from Lancaster No. 4 signalbox on August 12 1961, as 'Princess Royal' 4-6-2 No. 46206 *Princess Marie Louise* prepares for the assault on Lancaster bank with the 10am Glasgow-Euston (1M25). A 'Princess Royal' on this train was most unusual.

This was a superb vantage point — looking south from Lancaster No. 4 and I was particularly pleased with this photograph. Rebuilt 'Patriot' 4-6-0 No. 45522 *Prestatyn* leaves Lancaster with the 1.30pm Manchester Victoria-Glasgow of March 22 1963. The leading coaches are all LMS vehicles. Waiting in No. 2 bay is a Lancaster Green Ayre 2-6-4T with a local service for Morecambe.

Right: A northbound departure from Lancaster Castle, as seen from the up side of the line. With a pair of horseboxes behind the tender No. **46247** *City of Liverpool* **gets under way with the 9.20am Crewe-Perth (1S53) on March 15 1962.**

Another view south from the lofty Lancaster No. 4 signalbox. Stanier's first 'Pacific' No. 46200 *The Princess Royal* **hurries north on the down fast line through Castle station at the head of the 10.5am Euston-Perth (1S63) on March 16 1962. The line diverging to the right over the diamond crossing went to Glasson dock, whilst the branch on the left was the electrified Midland line to Green Ayre.**

Above: Stanier 8F 2-8-0 No. 48711, coupled to a narrow-sided Fowler tender, passes Lancaster on the down fast line with a 'Covhop' train — the 1.10pm Burn Naze-Corkickle of June 20 1964. 'Covhop' was the official description of a 'covered hopper.'

Below: The impressive view from the base of Lancaster No. 4 on June 8 1964, with Stanier Class 8P No. 46238 *City of Carlisle* leaving on the 2.54pm Preston-Barrow (1L21). The unusual appearance of a 'Duchess' on a Barrow train was arranged by Preston control . . .

Above: The double-track main line across Lancaster's Lune Bridge (known as Carlisle Bridge) was interlaced during reconstruction work in 1963 to give the civil engineering gang working clearances. No. 45317 treads cautiously over the bridge with the 1pm Carlisle-Warrington fast freight on February 26. Close inspection of the picture reveals the interlaced rails, which give the appearance of single track.

Reconstruction of the bridge opened up this new photographic location for a short period. 'Jubilee' 4-6-0 No. 45592 *Indore* crosses the Lune with the 5.10pm Manchester Exchange-Windermere (1L32) of July 25. Reconstruction involved the provision of a new deck on the original piers.

'Crab' 2-6-0 No. 42838 prepares to cross the River Lune over the Greyhound Bridge, from Lancaster Green Ayre station, with the 10.47am Leeds Morecambe of August 22 1961. Approaching Green Ayre from Morecambe is EMU No. M29024M. The 10mph speed restriction, uphill climb and sharp curve of this line from Green Ayre was a real test for drivers. This bridge now carries Lancaster's main road to the north.

Above: A very rare sighting at Lancaster Green Ayre during the afternoon of August 31 1962, as Class 04/8 2-8-0 No. 63837 of Immingham shed (40B) passes with the 8am special freight from Immingham to Heysham Moss. Once again, my thanks to the Control staff for making the necessary arrangements! Green Ayre station closed on January 3 1966.

Right: Approaching Scale Hall station on January 24 1964 is Fowler 4F 0-6-0 No. 44570 on the 12.40pm Heysham Moss-Tees ICI freight. The catenary equipment was the test section for BR's 25kv system. This stretch was known as 'The Golden Mile' because of the different types of experimental masts tested, as evident in this picture.

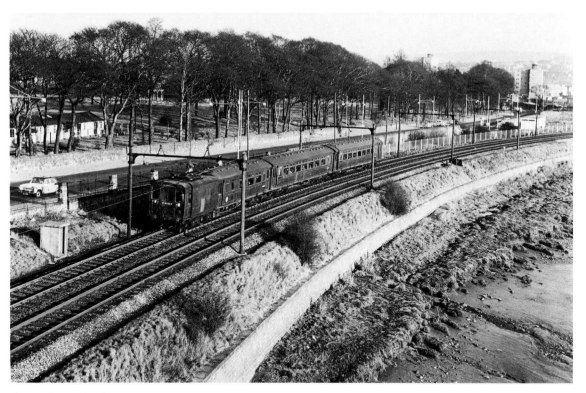

Above: The Midland line from Green Ayre to Morecambe Promenade, as seen from Carlisle bridge. EMU No. M28220M approaches Greyhound Bridge with the 2.10pm Morecambe-Lancaster Castle, January 24 1964. This trackbed is now a road.

Everything in this photograph has now gone. EMU No. 29023 pauses at Scale Hall station, between Morecambe Promenade and Lancaster, with the 12.40pm Morecambe-Lancaster Castle of September 23 1964. This station, opened by BR on June 8 1957 and closed in the Beeching plan on January 3 1966, must have been one of the shortest-lived on the railway.

Right: Once again, a railway scene which exists now in memory only. 'Crab' 2-6-0 No. 42888 marshalls the 11.13am Ladies Walk-Manvers Main Colliery empties at Ladies Walk Sidings, Lancaster on August 1 1963. This line was closed on January 3 1966 and this site is now occupied by small industrial units.

A view of New Zealand sidings from Skerton Bridge, Lancaster, June 30 1963. LMS 'Jinty' 0-6-0T No. 47651 approaches Green Ayre station with the 2.37pm Trip No. 72 to Lancaster Castle. Four other locomotives are visible. All you can see from here today is trees.

Above: To see this location today you would hardly believe this railway existed. Stanier 'Jubilee' 4-6-0 No. 45564 *New South Wales* passes New Zealand Sidings (left) and Ladies Walk Sidings (right) with the four-coach 7.17pm Morecambe Promenade-Leeds (2N71) of July 30 1963.

Left: Stanier 'Black 5' 4-6-0 No. 44672 leaves Ladies Walk en-route to Leeds with the 2.46pm from Morecambe Promenade (2N71) of June 15 1963. The train is seen running behind Lancaster's Lansil factory.

THE GLASSON DOCK BRANCH

Above: Lancaster's other branch linked the WCML with the city's own quay and also with Glasson Dock at the mouth of the River Lune. Ivatt 2MT 2-6-0 No. 46422 shunts empty vans into Williamson's factory on Lancaster quay on March 11 1964.

Above: No. 46422 propels withdrawn Fowler 2-6-4T No. 42301 into the shipbreakers scrapyard at Glasson Dock, five miles from Lancaster, on March 11 1964. Opened in 1878, the Glasson Dock branch closed to passengers at this tiny station on July 5 1930, and closed completely on September 7 1964.

This RCTS brake-van special traversed the five-mile Glasson Dock branch on June 20 1964, hauled by Ivatt 2MT 2-6-0 No. 46433, seen here passing Conder Green. The train comprises four BR and two LMS 20-ton brake vans, weighing 120 tons in all.

Left: This was a very unusual occurrence at Glasson Dock. Ivatt No. 46422 propels five-plank wagons of nitro-chalk from Heysham Moss onto the quay for shipment, March 2 1962. The floating cafe in the canal basin on the left is still in operation today.

Ivatt 2MT 2-6-0 No. 46422 runs cautiously over the weed covered track at Glasson Dock on March 2 1962, after working a train of nitro-chalk to the quay, for shipment. (See page 25). In the background stands the sailing ship *Moby Dick*, which was eventually destroyed by fire at Morecambe.

NORTH OF LANCASTER

A Stanier Class 8P in full cry. With a clear exhaust, No. 46250 *City of Lichfield* speeds north towards Morecambe South Junction with 'The Lakes Express' (1L27) of August 31 1963. The 'Duchess' was accelerating away from a stop at Lancaster.

Joining the WCML at Morecambe South Junction on June 3 1961 is grimy 'Black 5' No. 45427, of Carnforth shed (24L), with the 4.55pm non-corridor Morecambe Euston Road-Lancaster Castle.

Above: A wide variety of traffic and motive power was always on offer at Morecambe South Junction — and freight traffic was intense. 'Patriot' 4-6-0 No. 45501 *St Dunstan's* steams south on June 3 1961 with the 8.47am Carlisle-Ince Moss freight.

Stanier 2-8-0 No. 48386 awaits assistance between Bare Lane and Morecambe South Junction after stalling with 4P20 — the 6.12pm Heysham Moss-Darwen oil train, May 9 1967 'Black 5' No. 45450 arrived to assist the train, which weighed more than 700 tons.

Above: 'Black 5' No. 45448 blasts up the 1 in 100 incline from Bare Lane to Morecambe South Junction with the 3.10pm Heysham Harbour-Farington freight of February 5 1962.

Below: Viewed from Morecambe South Junction signal box, 5MT No. 45197 heads north with 'The Royal Scot' (9.5am Euston-Glasgow) on February 5 1962, in place of a failed EE Type 4 diesel.

HEST BANK

Above: As might be expected, the ubiquitous 'Black 5' could turn up on just about any duty. On May 28 1960 Carnforth's No. 44709 works the 1pm Workington-Manchester Victoria, at Hest Bank.

The West Coast Main Line at Hest Bank was a superb location to see trains running at high speeds. In this view, grubby Riddles 'Britannia' No. 70019 *Lightning* heads south with meat for Smithfield Market — the 1pm Carlisle-Broad Street of September 15 1963 (4A08).

Above: This is one of my favourite pictures, taken in a little-photographed location. 'Crab' 2-6-0 No. 42836 hurries south at Hest Bank with an up relief on August 1 1960.

Left: Hest Bank again, this time on July 6 1963. Fowler 2-6-4T No. 42319, at the head of a rake of LMS stock, steams south with the 3.15pm Windermere - Liverpool Exchange (1K47).

Right: 'Patriot' 4-6-0s became more common on the WCML in this area after 1965, when a batch were transferred to Lancaster Green Ayre (24J). On October 10 1961 No. 45510 races south at Hest Bank with the 10.30 Carlisle-Red Bank.

Below: Riddles 'Britannia' Pacific No. 70052 *Firth of Tay*, coupled to a BRID high capacity tender speeds past Hest Bank with the 10.50am Glasgow-Manchester Victoria of June 18 1961.

Above: The aftermath of the major mishap of May 20 1965, when the 10.10pm Glasgow-Kensington (1V42) was derailed at Hest Bank. Stanier 8F 2-8-0 No. 48199 marshalls damaged sleeping cars in readiness for transfer to Morecambe Balloon Carriage Sidings, on June 21 1965.

Left: Hest Bank station on July 13 1964. Leaving the up platform is Riddles 4MT 4-6-0 No. 75048 with the seven-coach 3.15pm Windermere - Liverpool Exchange (1K47). No. 75048 was allocated to Bank Hall, Liverpool at this time.

Above: A busy spell at Hest Bank station on October 3 1964, as Carnforth shed's Fowler 2-6-4T No. 42322 pauses with the 3.15pm Windermere Town-Lancaster (2P83). This station closed to passengers on February 3 1969, though the signal box, just visible beyond the footbridge, survives as a level crossing frame.

'Britannia' No. 70042 *Lord Roberts* sprints through Hest Bank station, working the 9.53pm Willesden-Carlisle parcels of March 4 1965. The 20-ton goods brake van in the middle of the train was provided for the guard as it was equipped with a coal-burning stove. The rear vehicle is a Gresley BG. Although closed in 1969, the station platforms survived until electrification of the WCML in the early 1970s.

Above: Hest Bank is the only place on the 401¼-mile London-Glasgow West Coast Main Line where the railway actually runs next to the sea — and only then for about ¼-mile! Here we see Stanier 'Mogul' No. 42945 on the seaside stretch with the 6am Carlisle-Bescot mixed of June 20 1961. The left-hand track gives access to Morecambe for southbound WCML trains, from a crossover and junction at Hest Bank station.

The single line connection from Hest Bank to Bare Lane forms a triangle with the WCML (seen in the background) and the Bare Lane-Morecambe South Junction double track section. Running from Hest Bank towards Bare Lane on June 23 1964 are 'Jinty' 0-6-0Ts Nos. 47599 and 47616 (both from Carnforth shed) on the 2.30pm Carnforth-Heysham Harbour (T84). The train is largely made up of 'Oxfit' cattle wagons for the Harbour and ICI tank wagons for Heysham Moss.

BARE LANE
MORECAMBE

Above: Outside the peak holiday periods the *TSS Duke of Lancaster,* which plied mainly between Heysham and Belfast, was used as a cruise ship to the Scottish isles, Scandinavia and Portugal. Trains connecting with these services ran from London, and in this view Stanier 'Jubilee' 4-6-0 No. 45613 *Kenya* hauls a return Holiday Cruise special from Heysham Harbour to Euston at Bare Lane, Morecambe, on May 28 1963.

Relaying the up main line at Bare Lane: snowplough-fitted Lancaster-Green Ayre 'Austerity' 2-8-0 No. 90706 propels engineers ballast wagons over the newly laid track on March 26 1961.

Morecambe versus Chester: 'Jubilee' No. 45696 *Arethusa* — with Fowler tender — storms through Bare Lane with a football special en route to Chester on December 8 1961. The seaside town could not resist advertising its attractions on the 'Jubilee's' smokebox door!

Top: Coupled to a motley selection of rolling stock, unrebuilt 'Patriot' 4-6-0 No. 45513 waits near Bare Lane for acceptance onto the WCML at Morecambe South Junction, on March 5 1961, with the 9.25am Heysham Harbour to Manchester Victoria parcels. The single line to the right is the connection from Bare Lane to Hest Bank.

Above: Collecting the single line token at Bare Lane for the section to Hest Bank. 'Jinty' 0-6-0Ts Nos. 47616 and 47599 lead the 12.25 Morecambe-Carnforth freight (T84) over the level crossing adjacent to the station on June 23 1964.

Above: The view from our landing window in the station house at Bare Lane just before lunchtime on March 8 1960. Fowler 2-6-4T No. 42409 — a Leeds Holbeck engine — approaches the platforms with the 11.21am Morecambe-Carnforth freight.

Left: A sunny morning between Bare Lane and Morecambe South Junction on February 9 1963 and Ivatt 4MT 2-6-0 No. 43124, with self cleaning smokebox, runs under clear signals towards the WCML with three non-corridor coaches forming the 9.55am Morecambe Promenade to Lancaster Castle passenger.

Right: Begrimed Ivatt 2MT 2-6-0 No. 46441 — now preserved at Steamtown, Carnforth in much cleaner condition — is ready for departure from Bare Lane station with the 4.55pm ex-Lakeside 'Lake Windermere Cruise' of August 9 1965. The train is a mixture of LMS and Mk 1 stock.

MORECAMBE
EUSTON ROAD

Morecambe Euston Road was the LNWR terminus at the seaside resort and was located approximately ¾-mile short of the existing Promenade station. Euston Road closed for normal passenger services in September 1958, but remained open for summer season trains until the mid '60s. This view, on September 7 1961, shows Ivatt 4MT 2-6-0 No. 43117 with the 11.48am service to Lancaster Castle. This site is now occupied by homes for senior citizens.

Above: The Euston Road station staff and Stanier 2-6-4T No. 42589 on August 24 1961. My father, Arthur Herbert — second from the left — was Euston Road's Station Master at this time. The train was the 11.48am to Lancaster Castle.

Below: Fairburn 2-6-4T No. 42136, framed by the impressive signal gantry at Euston Road's station throat, crosses to the up main line with the three-coach non-corridor 9.55am Morecambe Promenade - Lancaster Castle of September 11 1961. This loco spent its entire life at Lancaster Green Ayre shed.

CARNFORTH

The impressive layout at Carnforth No. 1 Junction on May 14 1963 is the setting for another favourite photograph. English Electric Type 4 diesel No. D303 works south with the 6.35pm Kendal — Euston parcels 1A65. A Gresley BG is immediately behind the engine.

Above: Carlisle Kingmoor Shed's 'Black 5' No. 44669 enters the down main line platform at Carnforth on May 23 1963 at the head of the 8am additional freight to Carlisle yard. Rationalisation over the years has radically altered this scene — even the main line platforms no longer exist.

An unusual visitor to Carnforth shed (10A) on September 19 1966 was withdrawn LNER A4 Pacific No. 60026 *Miles Beevor*, en-route to Crewe Works behind Stanier 8F No. 48346. Parts of No. 60026 were used in the overhaul of No. 60007 *Sir Nigel Gresley*, following its purchase by the A4 Locomotive Society.

Above: Pre-Steamtown days at Carnforth MPD. Locomotives visible in this overall view from the top of the coaling plant are Nos. 46499, 43103, 43066, 45328 and 48536. Another group of engines are visible in Keer Sidings, at the north end of the shed. July 2 1966.

Right: It's July 2 1966 and standing on the ashpit at 10A are Stanier 5MTs Nos. 45328 and 45092, and Stanier 8F 2-8-0 No. 48556.

Dramatic lighting at the south end of Carnforth shed on September 12 1964 highlights 'Black 5' No. 45156 *Ayrshire Yeomanry* and Riddles 'Britannia' Pacific No. 70023 *Venus*.

Right: Former Carnforth Driver Ronnie 'Blackie' Nelson and Fairburn 2-6-4T No. 2073 at 10A on June 1 1969, after the end of BR steam and by which time the Fairburn had been privately purchased and restored in LNWR 'blackberry black' livery. The loco is now on the Lakeside & Haverthwaite Railway.

Below: With its chimney sacked over, snowplough-fitted Fowler 4F 0-6-0 No. 44300 awaits winter weather and a return to duty at Carnforth shed on November 15 1964.

Above: Having arrived on the down main line at Furness & Midland Junction, 'Jinty' 0-6-0Ts Nos. 47375 and 47599 prepare to set back to Carnforth East Junction with the 12.28am Heysham Moss — Carnforth freight (T84) of May 25 1964.

Below: The stone crushing plant at Silverdale provides a backdrop to Stanier 8F 2-8-0 No. 48055 as it storms towards Carnforth with the 1.25pm freight from Workington (9L92) on May 21 1963.

Right: Borwick station, on the Carnforth-Wennington line on May 25 1964. Here we see 'Black 5' 4-6-0 No. 44893 passing the overgrown platforms with the 10.35 Carnforth-Leeds express, comprised entirely of LMS stock. Borwick closed on September 12 1960 and is now a private residence.

Below 'Crab' 2-6-0 No. 42812 begins the long climb to Clapham at Wennington Junction on September 20 1963 with the 2.50pm Heysham Harbour-Stourton fully-fitted freight. Wennington Junction was a busy location where trains divided for Carnforth and Lancaster and Morecambe. Also visible are the down running loop and refuge siding, now lifted.

EAST TO HELLIFIELD

Another 'Crab' 2-6-0. No. 42798, forges through the once-elegant station at Hellifield with the 2.50pm Heysham Harbour-Stourton fitted freight of September 14 1961. The engine shed coaling stage is visible in the background.

CARNFORTH-CARLISLE

Above: Yealand Conyers, situated between Carnforth and Burton & Holme on the West Coast Main Line, June 16 1963. English Electric Type 4 No. D 377 starts the long haul to Grayrigg with the 11.15am Birmingham - Glasgow (1S61).

Right: The double-track picturesque Windermere branch was heavily used in the summer months, but surprisingly it never seemed to attract many photographers. Riddles 4MT 4-6-0 No. 75060 attacks the fearsome 1 in 80 gradient from Kendal to Oxenholme with the 3.15pm Windermere - Liverpool Exchange of June 25 1964.

50

Above: Stanier Class 8P No. 46248 *City of Leeds* leaves Oxenholme and gets to grips with Grayrigg bank, hauling the 11.15pm Birmingham-Glasgow on October 4 1961. The Windermere branch slopes away to the right, from the platforms.

Below: The glorious scenery of the Lune Gorge before the intrusion of the M6. 'Austerity' 2-8-0s Nos. 90366 and 90328 rumble towards Dillicar with the 8am Fazakerley-Southwaite prefabricated track train of May 4 1963.

Above: 'EE' Type 4 No. D273 sprints over the Dillicar water troughs in the snow-covered Lune Gorge with the 10.5am Glasgow - Birmingham of November 18 1962. The 13-coach train is a mixture of LMS and BR Mk. 1 stock.

Right: A rainy evening at Tebay as 'Black 5' No. 45021 digs in with the 10.55am Oxley - Carlisle fitted freight of October 5 1963. There are four miles of 1 in 75 climb ahead and judging by the leaking steam, the 4-6-0 is far from its best.

This was the sort of picture that made all the failures worthwhile. Due to a derailment at Stainforth Sidings, on the Settle-Carlisle line on May 9 1963, all Midland line services were diverted via Shap. Low Gill and Clapham. Here we see the fireman on 'Black 5' No. 45313 enjoying the ride downgrade towards Tebay with the diverted 2.50pm Long Meg-Widnes, while up the hill towards Shap Wells comes No. 45329 with the 1.25pm Crewe-Carlisle fitted freight.

Running under clear LNWR lower quadrant signals at Thrimby Grange on May 9 1963 is an English Electric Type 4 No. D 384 with the 10.5am Glasgow-Birmingham (1M24).

Left: With the summit in sight, grubby 'Austerity' 2-8-0 No. 90157 steams steadily uphill at Shap Wells with the 'Tebay ballast' assisted at the rear by one of Tebay's 2-6-4Ts, No. 42414, on June 16 1962, a beautiful clear day.

Right: With the tender tank topped up, Stanier 'Black 5' 4-6-0 No. 45094 gets away from Penrith on May 8 1963 with the 2.4pm Carlisle - Ravenhead Junction freight. A 'water stop' at Penrith for southbound trains was frequently a subterfuge for a 'blow-up'!

Above: A classic country station scene in the Lake District which is now no more. The Station Master closes the doors prior to departure of the 1.31pm Penrith-Workington DMU of June 9 1962. The Keswick-Workington section closed on April 18 1966 and the truncated Penrith-Keswick section followed it into oblivion on March 6 1972. Even the 'Yellow Diamond' DMU class is now extinct.

A busy spell at Carlisle Kingmoor MPD (12A) on September 26 1964. Stabled locomotives include Nos. 73079, 72005 *Clan Macgregor*, 61397, 61244 *Strang Steel* and 45082.

One of the centre roads at Carlisle Citadel is host to 'Jubilee' 4-6-0 No. 45697 *Achilles* and Riddles 'Clan' No. 72008 *Clan Macleod*. The 'Jubilee' was waiting to take over the 12.40pm Gourock-Leicester, London Road, while the 'Pacific' was ready to work the 4.40pm Carlisle-Hellifield. The date was August 7 1965.

MIXED TRAFFIC

Above: The Carlisle SLS/MLS railtour awaits the rightaway from Langholm, to Carlisle behind preserved North British Railway 'Glen' 4-4-0 No. 256 *Glen Douglas*, April 6 1963. This railtour also visited Carlisle 'new' yard at Kingmoor, prior to its opening.

Right: A sunny evening at the trackside near the Express Dairy, Appleby, on May 9 1963. Stanier 5MT 4-6-0 No. 45126 hurries through Appleby West with the 11.55am Brewery - Carlisle mixed freight.

Above: An idyllic image of the country railway, on the North Eastern line between Kirkby Stephen and Penrith. Ivatt 4MT 2-6-0 No. 43023 approaches Appleby East with the 2.40pm Warcop-Carlisle Yard freight of May 3 1963. Scenes like this were typical victims of the Beeching axe.

Centre, left: Industrial steam abounded but was rarely photographed, in comparison with BR steam. This shed grouping at Walkden Colliery on September 17 1964 depicts three Hunslet 'Austerity' 0-6-0STs, one of which is fitted with a Giesl exhaust ejector. A fourth saddletank is just visible under cover beyond the coal wagons on the left.

Below, left: Also at Walkden on the same day: North Staffordshire 0-6-2T No. 2 (built 1922) which was still in traffic at this time. This loco was withdrawn by the LMS in 1937 as No. 2271 and sold to Walkden Collieries, where it was named *Princess*, and continued in service until 1966. The NSR livery was applied for an exhibition in 1958. No. 2 was stored at Shugborough Hall, Staffordshire from 1966 until early 1984, when it was moved to the Mining Museum at Chatterley Whitfield, for static display.

YORK

Approaching Holgate Road bridge on August 7 1961 is Riddles 9F 2-10-0 No. 92116 with a day excursion to Scarborough. The train includes Thompson, Gresley and Stanier stock.

Running neck and neck towards York station at Holgate Road on August 7 1961 are Thompson B1 4-6-0 No. 61023 *Hirola* and Stanier 'Black 5' No. 45268, which is also working a day excursion to Scarborough.

Above: Near-perfect photographic conditions on the south side of Holgate Road bridge, near York station, on August 7 1961. Gresley V2 2-6-2 No. 60961, of York shed, leaves with an up express for King's Cross.

Left: Two-tone green liveried Class 55 'Deltic' No. D 9007 *Pinza* heads south through York with the up 'Flying Scotsman' of August 7 1961. The picture pre-dates the day of the overall yellow warning panel and the locomotive was in immaculate condition.

Above: With the regulator closed and steam roaring from the safety valves, Stanier 5MT No. 45445 drifts towards York, at Holgate Road bridge, en-route to Scarborough on August 7 1961 with a Holiday Express from Barrow-in-Furness, as the enormous headboard proudly proclaims. I wonder what they thought in Scarborough!

Above: The jet of steam under the centre driving wheels shows the sanders are in action on LNER A4 Pacific No. 60034 *Lord Faringdon*, which is at the head of a Newcastle-King's Cross express at York on August 7 1961. The loco was allocated to King's Cross — better known as 'Top Shed'.

Right: Despite the fact that it was taken away from my 'home' patch, this picture near Holgate Bridge remains one of my favourites. In beautiful conditions, Thompson B1 4-6-0 No. 61053 makes a vigorous exit from York with a semi-fast to Sheffield, August 7 1961.

Above: A rare catch for me at the Holgate Road ticket platforms on August 7 1961: LNER B16 4-6-0 No. 61455, in charge of a 12-coach excursion including 11 LMS coaches. Note the condemned Gresley stock in the background.

Right: In their last days the A4s were transferred to the Glasgow - Aberdeen services and I spent a happy weekend photographing them on these duties. Here is No. 60004 *William Whitelaw* at Perth MPD (63A), being prepared to work the 5.10pm Perth-Carstairs of May 9 1965.

ON SHED

Left: Immingham B1 4-6-0 No. 61168 prepares to take coal at Sheffield Darnall shed, (41A) April 8 1962.

Above: A classic image of the working railway at Sheffield Darnall on April 8 1962. Work-stained Thompson B1 4-6-0 No. 61282 is stabled in front of Gresley V2 2-6-2 No. 60956. Power for the B1's electric lights was provided by the steam driven generator seen on the running plate, alongside the smokebox.

With its running fox motif still in place on the boiler cladding, No. 60017 *Silver Fox* stands in the cinders at Gateshead shed (52A) on April 24 1960. This was another 'top shed' engine.

SCOTLAND

Right: The Glasgow & South Western station at Ayr was an impressive backdrop for steam photographs. Riddles 3MT 2-6-0 No. 77017 of Hurlford shed (67B) waits to depart with the 6.43pm working to Glasgow of 16 July 1962.

Below: The teatime local to Ballachulish stands under the overall roof at Oban on April 27 1961, with McIntosh '19' class 2P 0-4-4T No. 55124 at its head. This locomotive was the sole survivor of its class, introduced in 1895. This roof is now said to be unsafe and these tracks have been lifted in recent years.

Almost at the end of steam in Scotland. Taken on May 8 1965, Riddles 'Britannia' No. 70041 *Sir John Moore* strides away from Stirling with the 9.25am Crewe-Perth (1S53). Note the Caledonian Railway lattice signal posts.

Oban, April 27 1961, and Stanier 'Black 5' 4-6-0 No. 45366 stands ahead of the stop blocks with the early morning arrival from Glasgow Buchanan street.

WALES

Above: This is how I like to remember the GWR. Running under clear signals at Ruabon on August 16 1961 is Collett 5700 class 0-6-0PT No. 3689, bound for Llangollen.

Right: The classic GWR branch line train. Collett 14XX 0-4-2T No. 1432 is paired with an auto-coach at Wrexham Central station on October 11 1960.

Above: Moat Lane Junction — change for Llanidloes, Rhayader, Builth Wells, Brecon and South Wales. No. 7822 *Foxcote Manor* draws into the now extinct station with an up freight on August 15 1961. This station closed on December 31 1962 — just over a year after this photograph was taken — but the 'Manor' lives on in preservation.

Below: The 'Cambrian Coast Express' leaves Moat Lane Junction behind Machynlleth shed's immaculately turned out 'Manor' 4-6-0 No. 7803 *Barcote Manor* on August 15 1961. This train was a through service from Paddington to Aberystwyth and Pwllheli.

Above: With the tender piled high with coal, No. 7803 *Barcote Manor* stands fully prepared at Aberystwyth shed, prior to working the 'Cambrian Coast Express' of August 15 1961. It was not unusual for engines working this train to be turned out in such pristine condition. This building is now the engine shed for the 1ft 11½in gauge Vale of Rheidol Railway 2-6-2Ts.

A busy scene outside Machynlleth shed (89C) on August 14 1961. The down 'Cambrian Coast Express' approaches the platforms behind 'Manor' 4-6-0s Nos. 7816 *Frilsham Manor* and 7811 *Dunley Manor*. The train divided here and Riddles 2-6-2T No. 82006, standing in the down loop with a Stanier BSK, worked the rear portion to Pwllheli.

Above: The original V of R engine shed at Aberystwyth, which was on the banks of the Afon Rheidol, with No. 9 *Prince of Wales* being prepared for duty, August 15 1961. Note the coal on the tank top, for these locos are now oil-burners.

Left: Three Cocks Junction on October 10 1962 — just two months before closure. Ivatt 2MT 2-6-0 No. 46503 stands in the station platform with the 12.40pm Hereford-Three Cocks Junction working. This was once a busy junction of lines from Moat Lane Junction, Brecon and Hereford: all three routes closed on December 31 1962.

Home was in the north but I made many trips to the Southern in pursuit of steam, and this photograph was taken during a visit to the Swanage branch. Rebuilt Bulleid 'Merchant Navy' Pacific No. 35021 *New Zealand Line* brakes for its Wareham stop on the 11.30am Weymouth-Waterloo of October 22 1963.

SOUTHERN
STEAM

Above: Drummond M7 0-4-4T No. 30107 takes water at Wareham after arriving with the 11.40am from Swanage of October 22 1963. This branch survived until closure on January 3 1972 and it is now the subject of a preservation plan.

Left: One of the few surviving Maunsell S15 4-6-0s, No. 30837, of Feltham shed (70B), leaves Eastleigh yard with an up freight, October 24 1963.

Right: An everyday picture of Southern steam in its last years: 'N' Class 2-6-0 No. 31405 stands in the sun alongside the coaling stage at Eastleigh (71A) on June 10 1965.

Below: With a clear road ahead from Bournemouth Central, a full head of steam and one minute to departure time, the driver of No. 35019 *French Line CGT* tops up the tank while the fireman pulls coal forward onto the shovelling plate. The train is the 10.8am Bournemouth West - Waterloo, October 22 1963.

Left: The signals are off and No. 34025 *Whimple* awaits the guard's right-away with the 10.50am Bournemouth West-York of June 9 1965.

Below: Riddles Class 5 4-6-0 No. 73043 gets away from Bournemouth Central with the 10am Bournemouth West - Liverpool Lime Street of June 10 1965. Rebuilt Bulleid 'West Country' Pacific No. 34024 *Tamar Valley* waits on one of the centre roads with an ECS train.

Crossing the road entrance to Southampton pier on May 3 1961 is LBSC Billinton E4 0-6-2T No. 32556, with a yard-to-yard transfer freight. This class was introduced in 1897.

THE ISLE OF WIGHT

Six months before the end of steam working on the Isle of Wight system. Adams LSWR Class 02 0-4-4T No. 35 *Freshwater* hauls six non-corridor coaches forming the 2.25pm Ryde Pier-Ventnor of June 7 1965. Originally introduced in 1889, the 02s were fitted with Westinghouse brake equipment in 1923.

Left: No. 35 *Freshwater* makes a brisk departure from Ryde St. Johns with the 12.18 Ryde Pier-Cowes of June 7 1965. Another of the IOW's great attractions was the vintage rolling stock, clearly seen in this view.

Below: Within a year of this photograph being taken, this Victorian railway had gone. Here we see 02 No. 16 *Ventnor*, in comparatively clean condition, standing at Ventnor with the 17.42 to Ryde Pier, June 7 1965. The Ventnor - Shanklin route closed on April 4 1966.

Left: Approaching Smallbrook Junction on June 7 1965 is 02 0-4-4T No. 29 *Alverstone* with the 1.18pm Ryde Pier-Cowes service. The Smallbrook Junction-Cowes section closed on February 21 1966.

Below: This was a brief visit to the Somerset & Dorset line, en-route home from a photographic expedition to Southern metals. On June 11 1965 the fireman of Ivatt 2MT 2-6-2T No. 41206 puts the 'bag' in at Evercreech Junction, whilst working bunker-first on a local freight to Templecombe.

EVERCREECH JUNCTION

Begrimed Riddles 4MT 4-6-0 No. 75073, of Penzance shed (83G) comes to a stand at Evercreech Junction on June 11 1965 with the 3.20pm Bath Green Park-Bournemouth West working, comprised of Bulleid stock.

THE ISLE OF MAN

Above: The Isle of Man Railway is a long standing favourite and I have visited it many times. The line's unique character and appeal are clear in this picture of a three-coach Ramsey branch train arriving at Douglas on August 7 1963, behind 2-4-0T No. 5 *Mona*. The need for extensive track repairs prompted closure of the Ramsey branch in 1968.

Below: This is now a car park! Beyer Peacock 2-4-0T No. 10 *G. H. Wood* (works No. 4662 of 1905) prepares to pilot a Ramsey-Douglas train at St Johns, which also closed in 1968. Probably few of the visitors who park their cars here today realise that the railway ever existed.

Above: A typical IOMR scene of the early 1960s as 2-4-0T No. 11 *Maitland* (works No. 4663 of 1905) prepares to leave Castletown with a Douglas — Port Erin train, June 17 1960. The IOMR lorry was collecting parcels. This section is still open — and little changed today.

The ex-County Donegal Railway Walker Brothers bogie diesel railcars Nos. 19/20 (built 1950/51) leave St Johns, en-route to Kirk Michael, on August 8 1963. These railcars, bought by the IOMR in 1961 are retained in working order today to cover in the event of steam failures.

Above: 2-4-0T No. 6 *Peveril* (built 1875) takes water at Peel on June 17 1960, having worked in from Douglas. The Peel branch, from St Johns, also closed in 1968 when major track renewal became necessary.

Right: Douglas station, June 17 1960. 2-4-0T No. 13 *Kissack* (works No. 5382 of 1910) awaits departure for Ramsey. My father, Arthur Herbert, is standing next to the open door with his copy of the 'Bradshaw' timetable. He never went anywhere without it! The overall station roof has since been dismantled.

BROMSGROVE

Above: Bromsgrove, at the foot of the notorious Lickey Incline, on July 14 1962. Coasting off the 1 in 37 gradient with safety valves blowing is Stanier 'Black 5' 4-6-0 No. 44660 with a relief Birmingham New Street-Bournemouth West service. Note the pigeon baskets on the up platform.

A combined potential tractive effort of more than 62,000 lbs storms through Bromsgrove station to do battle with the Lickey incline on July 14 1962. Hawksworth 94XX 0-6-0PT No. 8402 and Riddles 9F 2-10-0 No. 92079 were giving vigorous assistance to Riddles 5MT 4-6-0 No. 73003 with 'The Pines Express'. I shall never forget the sound these two locomotives made!

IRELAND

Right: Ireland's 5ft. 3in. gauge system was an irresistible draw for me from 1961 and in 1964 — as the end approached — I was making the crossing about once a month. Unusual machines were always a characteristic of the Irish scene and here we see derelict GNR crane tank No. 31 in the scrap road at Inchicore Works, Dublin, on July 28 1964.

Below: On July 28 1964, GNR class VS 4-4-0 No. 207 *Boyne* is turned at Dublin Amiens Street shed, having arrived with a day excursion from Belfast. No. 207, built in Manchester by Beyer Peacock in 1948, was painted in blue livery and looked magnificent.

Above: The Irish also had their own distinctive approach to the railbus principle, as this converted road vehicle at Inchicore Works illustrates! It is GNR railcar No. 8177 and was photographed on October 22 1961.

Left: More examples of the Irish railbus builders art at Inchicore, also pictured on October 22 1961. The vehicle was operated by the CIE — though how successfully is not recorded! The flat wagon behind the railbus is carrying a narrow gauge railcar cab — it is not a double-deck railbus prototype as might first appear!

Right: Northern Counties Committee (NCC) Class WT 2-6-4T No. 53 stands in the station yard at Warrenpoint on August 2 1964 with the empty stock of a day excursion from Belfast Great Victoria Street, which is now closed. These engines were Derby built — and it shows. The locos were shipped in sections to Northern Ireland, via Heysham.

Below: Portadown MPD, on the Belfast-Dublin line, on August 9 1964. The loco in the foreground is class 'U' 4-4-0 No. 67 *Louth*.

Above: This was the sort of picture which enticed me back to Ireland again and again — if only it were the same today! This is Strabane on May 20 1964, with GNR 'S' class 4-4-0 No. 60 *Slieve Donard* on station pilot duty. The remains of the County Donegal Joint Railway station is visible in the background.

Left: An almost timeless scene at Dungannon, on the GNR main line from Belfast to Londonderry on July 18 1963. GNR 'S' class 4-4-0 No. 170 *Errigal* stands alongside a magnificent water column and signal with the 3pm Belfast Great Victoria Street - Londonderry Foyle Road service.

Above: NCC Class 'W' 2-6-0 No. 91 *The Bush* stands in the sun outside the GNR loco shed at Londonderry on March 21 1964. Note the apparatus on the cab side for catching tablets used on single line sections. These engines were built between 1933 and 1942 by the LMS at Derby.

Right: Shunting in the GNR Londonderry goods yard on July 18 1963 is GNR Class 'SG2' 0-6-0 No. 52, one of a class built between 1913 and 1924 by Clifford. The tender has a distinct LMS family resemblance.

Left: Inside Belfast Transport Museum. The loco is NCC Class 'U2' 4-4-0 No. 74 *Dunluce Castle*, built by the North British Locomotive Company, at Glasgow, in 1924. Withdrawn from service in 1961, the 4-4-0 was donated by the Ulster Transport Authority to the Museum, where it is still on show today.

Below: Belfast Adelaide MPD. Standing amongst the piles of ashes on August 3 1964 are NCC Class 'W' 2-6-0 No. 91 *The Bush* and GNR Class 'SG3' 0-6-0 No. 47. Pictures like this epitomise the appeal of Irish steam.

SPAIN & ITALY

Above: I also travelled to Europe for the sole purpose of photographing steam, and Spain's 5ft. 6in. gauge locomotives were an impressive and distinctive breed. On the right, 4-8-2 No. 241F2110 tops up with sand at Miranda de Ebro on September 27 1967, alongside 4-8-4 No. 242-2008. Both locomotives are fitted with standard RENFE electric headlights.

Right: On January 21 1967, 0-6-0T No. 851.107 shunts vans on the dock at Syracuse, Southern Sicily, in front of quayside tenements. This was an Italian State Railways locomotive.

Sunday afternoon at Madrid Delicias roundhouse, September 30 1967. Stabled on shed are (left to right): 2-8-2 No. 141F2330; 4-8-0 No. 240F2610; 4-8-0 No. 240F2561 and 4-8-0 No. 240F2599. The corrugated roofed trolley was used by shed fitters for moving their welding equipment about!

'The Fleche D'Or' — the French connecting service of 'The Golden Arrow' — crosses the River Liane at Boulogne on May 18 1965 behind 'Pacific' No. 231E17. This train was booked to leave Calais at 2.37pm, bound for Paris Nord.

FRANCE & GERMANY

Below: A majestic sight at Boulogne, also on May 18 1965, as 'Liberator' 2-8-2s Nos. 141R348 and 141R311 run light-engines to the shed.

Left: Koblenz, Deutches Bundesbahn, September 29 1965. The guard of the 2.36pm to Paris East gives details of the train formation to the driver of '01' Pacific No. 01.059. With his green uniform, red sash and braided cap, the guard cut an impressive figure.

Below: Class 50 DB 2-10-0 No. 50.1919 stands on the turntable in the autumn sunshine at Munich MPD, September 25 1965. The locomotive had been towed out of the roundhouse courtesy of the shed staff, just for us to photograph it. The staff were pleasant and helpful and all the locos were shunted out one by one, for our cameras.

THE ROMNEY, HYTHE & DYMCHURCH RAILWAY

Above: The miniature main line of the RHDR remains a firm favourite and I have spent many happy hours at its tracksides. On May 21 1965 Yorkshire Engine Co. 'Pacific' No. 9 *Winston Churchill* (built 1931) is ready to depart from New Romney with a train for Hythe. Note the bell behind the chimney, which adds the finishing touch to the 'Pacific's' American outline.

Right: The elegant and beautifully proportioned lines of Davey Paxman 4-6-2 No. 7 *Typhoon* (built 1926) are evident in this low viewpoint picture at Hythe, May 21 1965.

Left: Davey Paxman 2-8-2 No. 1 *Green Goddess* (built 1925) drifts through Woodland near New Romney with the first train of the day on May 22 1965.

Below: There's not a speck of dirt or a wisp of stray steam to be seen from No. 7 *Typhoon*, pictured waiting to depart from Hythe with 'The Marshlander' of May 21 1965. The locomotive was immaculate and a real credit to its driver and the Railway. This was steam at its best: well cared-for and performing to perfection — it was in stark contrast to the sorry condition of the greater part of BR's surviving steam fleet at this time.

The end of steam on the Southern Region. Rebuilt Bulleid 'Merchant Navy' Pacific No. 35023 *Holland Afrika Line* stands at Weymouth with the 8.30am Waterloo-Weymouth of Saturday July 8 1967. This was the last full day of steam on the Southern and after this only the London Midland Region kept steam engines at work; by August 1968 they too had gone. I was in Traffic Control at this time and operationally steam had become a nightmare. Failures, shortages of steam and late running habitually resulted from the poor state of the engines and as a Controller I couldn't help sighing with relief when the last fires had been dropped. However, as a lover of steam I was as saddened as everyone else. The Working Railway would never be quite the same, ever again.